CONTENTS

GETTING BACK TO BASICS

❖ ❖ ❖ ❖

For generations, country folk lived, cherished, and passed down a straightforward approach to life: They made do with whatever materials and resources they had on hand, taking care of hearth and home using a handful of basic supplies, a dollop of down-home ingenuity, and a bit of good old-fashioned elbow grease. It was a commonsense, practical, frugal way of life—not always easy, but simple in the best sense of the word.

These days, we often find ourselves longing for that kind of simplicity. We're discovering that the fancy commercial products and tools developed to make our lives easier have in many ways made them more complicated. We're beginning to wonder whether the powerful cleansers and

other newfangled chemicals we use are poisoning our land, our water, and our children. We're growing alarmed at the mountains of plastics and other waste generated by our endless quest to try the latest miracle product. And while we've taken enthusiastic advantage of pricey, labor-saving devices, we're coming to realize that our lack of physical effort is leaving us out of shape, overweight, and unhealthy—not to mention poorer. Sometimes progress really isn't all it's cracked up to be.

That's why sensible people from cities and rural areas alike have begun to explore and adopt new, less-wasteful, and healthier approaches to everyday chores. And where are they finding the inspiration and know-how for many of these "new" approaches? In the proud and practical traditions of old-time country living. They are rediscovering the wisdom—not to mention many of the tools and practices—that previous generations of country folk relied upon: letting nothing go to waste; finding new and creative uses for basic supplies; breathing new life into used goods; and putting in the effort necessary to create clean, healthy, comfortable homes for themselves and their families.

Those "new old ways" from the country are just what you'll find in this book. It's a treasure trove of simple, practical, inexpensive solutions for daily challenges such as ridding bathroom surfaces of soap residue and mildew; clearing slow-running drains; polishing wood furniture; cleaning soiled walls and floors; removing coffee, ink, and grease stains from clothing; brightening white linens; chasing pesky pests and varmints away; and handling lots of little chores around the house. The hints rely mostly on a few common household supplies—and the years of cleaning and do-it-yourself experience accumulated in country homes over dozens, even hundreds, of years. Many of the tips require nothing more harsh than lemon juice, white vinegar, and borax. (Of course, it's always best to err on the side of safety and protect yourself and your household furnishings by wearing rubber or vinyl gloves, donning protective eyewear if solutions could splash as you're mixing or using them, spot-testing even these home-made cleaning products on inconspicuous areas first, and ensuring good ventilation whenever called for in the directions.)

So read on to discover ingenious, old-time country ways to simplify your household chores—and your life.

CLEANING

❖ ❖ ❖ ❖

In generations past, country folk didn't have a cabinet full of all kinds of cleaning products for specific uses. They didn't select from shelves of cleansers, detergents, and specialized cleaning tools, nor would most of them have wasted their hard-earned money on such things. Yet they managed to keep clean, tidy homes. Here you'll find some of the time-tested tips and cleaning wisdom they relied on. Give them a try in your own home.

BATHROOM

 Don't throw away old nylon stockings. Rolled into a ball or slipped over an old but clean cotton sock that's been rolled into a ball, those nylons become excellent non-scratch scrubbers for cleaning the sink and tub.

 Soften up the soap scum that collects on the sides of your bathtub with baby oil (a generic variety will do just fine). Mix 1 part baby oil in 4 parts water, use a funnel to pour the mixture into a clean spray bottle, and spray the sides of the tub (but try not to spray directly on the bottom of the tub). Give the solution a few minutes to loosen the soap scum, then wipe it away using a clean, damp cloth or sponge. To remove any oil that may have gotten on the

Spray-Bottle Redux

Keep spray bottles from commercial preparations (or ask your neighbors for their empties), wash and rinse them thoroughly, and reuse them for your homemade cleaners. Just be sure to clearly label the spray bottles with their new contents.

bottom of the tub and made it slippery, wipe it down with a sponge soaked in white vinegar. (And as always, be sure to use caution when you are entering and exiting the tub.)

Pour a bit of 3 percent hydrogen peroxide on bathroom faucets and other fixtures to bubble away lime stains. Then rinse with plain water.

To remove stubbornly stuck-on soap residue and calcium stains from the bathtub, sink, and surrounding tiles, use a paste made of cream of tartar and 3 percent hydrogen peroxide: In a small container, mix just enough hydrogen peroxide into the cream of tartar to form a thick paste. Apply the paste directly to the scummy surface, and use a homemade nylon scrubber (as described previously) or a firm-bristled brush to scrub the surface with the paste. Then rinse clean and wipe dry.

To clean darkened grout, mix ¼ cup liquid bleach into 1 quart water, moisten an old toothbrush with the mixture, scrub the grout, then rinse with water.

Another inexpensive way to clean grout is to make a paste of 3 parts baking soda and 1 part water, scrub it into the grout using an old toothbrush, and rinse with water.

Funnel on the Cheap

When you mix a lot of your own household cleaning products, having funnels in various sizes is a godsend. It minimizes mess, prevents wasteful spills, and makes the whole process faster and easier. But don't use the money you saved on cleaning products to buy funnels. Make funnels for free by recycling the plastic jugs and bottles that milk, water, and other liquids are sold in. Once you've finished the original product, wash (if necessary), rinse, and dry the plastic container. Then, turn it upside down so the opening faces downward, and use a grease pencil or marker to mark where you want the top of the funnel to be. (Higher sides can help prevent splatters and overflows.) Next, use heavy-duty scissors or garden shears to cut the container in two at the height of your mark. The portion with the original opening (and the cap removed) is your new funnel. The remaining portion can be used to keep small lids in one place in a cupboard, to scoop birdseed from the bag, to collect stray hardware or pocket change, even to hold beneath the used funnel to catch drips. If you make your funnels out of gallon and quart jugs, water bottles, and other plastic beverage containers of various sizes, you're sure to have a funnel for every need.

Cheap, generic cola makes a great toilet-bowl cleaner. It can even help loosen those nasty hard-water stains. Just empty a can of cola into the bowl, let it work for about an hour, then scrub and flush. Use a sponge or cloth moistened with white vinegar to wipe off any sticky drops of cola that may have splattered onto the rim or other nearby surfaces. The vinegar will also clean and disinfect these surfaces.

You can say goodnight to a dirty toilet bowl by sprinkling some borax around the inside surface and into the bowl water itself before you go to bed. Then, in the morning, you'll be able to whisk away the stains easily with the swish of your toilet brush.

Natural Odor Killers

You're less likely to need pricey, artificial air fresheners in the bathroom if you allow sunshine and fresh air in as often as possible. Sunshine helps kill mold, while fresh, dry air can help evaporate moisture before it can lead to mildew and its unpleasant smell.

White vinegar can also be used as a toilet-bowl cleaner. Pour the vinegar down and around the inside of the bowl, and let it sit for 30 minutes or so. In the meantime, use a vinegar-dampened cloth to wipe down the top edge of the bowl and the top and bottom of the seat and lid. Then, take a toilet brush, sprinkle some baking soda on it, scrub any remaining stains on the inside of the bowl, and flush.

Help speed up a slow drain by first pouring ½ cup baking soda down it, then follow up with ¾ cup white vinegar. Don't bend over to watch this drain cleaner in action, though. These two substances, when combined, tend to foam and fizz, and even though this mixture is nontoxic, you still don't want it in your eyes. After about 20 minutes, flush the drain with very hot water.

Easy Drain Opener

When a sink drain has begun to back up, sometimes simply putting in the drain stopper, filling the sink full of water, and then suddenly pulling the plug creates enough pressure to dislodge a clog and get the drain moving again.

CARPETS, RUGS & FLOORS

 Get yourself a self-cleaning broom. A good old-fashioned broom made from real broomcorn actually cleans itself as you use it. Soil and dirt particles won't linger between the bristles the way they tend to do between newfangled synthetic broom bristles.

 Refresh a carpet or a large area rug that's absorbed unpleasant pet, smoke, or other smells by thoroughly mixing together 2 cups cornmeal with 1 cup borax and sprinkling the mix onto the carpet. After about an hour, vacuum the carpet. You'll be amazed at how much better the whole room smells.

 Cornstarch, sprinkled on liberally, left for an hour or so, and then vacuumed up, can also help to freshen a carpet or large area rug.

 A good spot cleaner for carpet stains is shaving cream. Take an old shaving brush or purchase a small, cheap paintbrush that you keep just for this purpose, and use it to work the shaving cream into the stain. Then use a clean, damp rag to wipe up the shaving cream and the remnants of the stain. Blot the area dry with a clean, white or color-fast cloth.

 Need to remove candle wax from carpet? Soak an old, clean piece of cloth with water, wring it out, and lay it on the wax. Set your iron to low heat, and run it over the cloth until all the wax has been transferred from the carpet to the cloth.

 To get rid of a grease stain on carpet, sprinkle the stain with finely sifted flour, lay a piece of brown paper (from a clean paper lunch bag or shopping bag, for example) over the stain, and stack phone books, bricks, or other heavy weight on the paper over the stain. Wait about half an hour. Remove the weight and the paper, then use a clean whisk broom to sweep the flour out of the carpet. Repeat the process as many times as necessary to soak up all the grease, using fresh flour and paper each time.

Beat 'Em!

Your throw rugs are great dust and dirt collectors, and a quick shake outside the back door may simply not be enough to knock out much of that soil, especially if the rugs are thick or braided. So try doing what country homemakers have done for ages: Hang your rugs on a laundry line or drape them over a fence, and use a broom or other stick to beat the dust out of them.

 Scuff marks on linoleum can often be removed with toothpaste, but be sure you use the old-fashioned paste form, not a gel. Use an old toothbrush to work the toothpaste into the mark, wipe it away with a damp cloth, then wash the floor as usual.

 If you spill grease on a wood floor, quickly pour a small amount of very cold water on it. This will cause the grease to harden and help keep it from penetrating the wood. Then immediately wipe up the grease and the water with a clean, dry rag.

FURNITURE

 Skip the expensive, store-bought sprays, oils, and creams, and try polishing your wood furniture with shoe polish instead. First, place the tin of polish in a warm spot in the kitchen or near the furnace to soften it so it will spread and penetrate easily. Then use a soft cloth to apply the polish and work it into the wood. Finally, use another soft cloth to buff the wood to a shine. Clear polish works with all woods. Lighter browns work well with walnut and similarly colored wood, and darker polish works better with darker woods. (It's always best to test the polish on an inconspicuous part of the furniture first to be sure you've got a good match.) The polish can even help fill in and/or hide minor scratches and nicks in the wood. You may not want to use the shoe polish (at least the colored varieties) on chair or bench surfaces that will come in direct contact with clothing, however, to avoid any color transfer or staining of clothes. If you do apply it to seating, work it in well, then thoroughly buff the wood before using the chair.

Plain olive oil, thoroughly rubbed in with a soft cloth, makes a handy polish for unpainted wood furniture.

 You can also create your own pleasant-smelling furniture polish by following this simple recipe: Combine ⅓ cup white vinegar with 1 cup baby oil. Use a soft cloth to thoroughly rub it into the wood. (If you're not a fan of baby-oil smell, use an unscented variety.)

 One of the best furniture-polishing cloths is something you wear on your feet. An old, laundered, cotton sock, slipped over your hand and perhaps treated with a bit of wood-furniture cleaner or polish, allows you to easily clean the crevices in carved-wood table and chair legs, banister supports, chair arms and back-slats, carved-wood

Baby Your Furniture

Don't give away or throw out socks that your baby or young child has outgrown. Dress your furniture's feet in them when you're cleaning or rearranging a room that has an uncarpeted floor; they'll help protect the floor's finish and make sliding the furniture easier.

accents, beveled edges, and more. It conforms to your hand and to whatever part of the furniture you are wiping, allowing for quicker and more thorough cleaning.

 A "handy" way of removing pet hair from upholstered sofas and chairs, bedspreads, and other soft furnishings is to put on a pair of rubber gloves (wear cotton glove liners if rubber tends to irritate your skin), dampen their outer surface, and wipe the fabric. (Rewet the outside of the gloves as necessary to maintain their "attractiveness.") You'll be happily surprised at their almost magnetic ability to pull the hairs off your furniture.

 Don't let a water ring ruin the look of a wood table. You can remove it easily with a little sandwich spread. With a clean, soft cloth, rub mayonnaise into the water mark on the wood. Leave it overnight. The next day, use another clean, soft cloth to wipe away the mayonnaise and, along with it, the water ring.

KITCHEN

For extra-greasy dishes, pots, and pans, add 3 to 4 table-spoons of white vinegar, along with a squirt of your usual dishwashing liquid, to a sinkful of hot water. Vinegar's natural acidity will cut through that stubborn grease like a knife through butter.

To help prevent spotting on wine glasses and other stem-ware after washing, give them a final rinse in a sink or basin filled with warm water and a cup of white vinegar. Then simply allow them to air dry.

Your family's traditional recipe for mouth-watering spa-ghetti sauce was passed down to you from your mother, who got it from her mother, who got it from her grand-mother, who came to this country from a distant land. Too bad it didn't come with instructions on preventing the stubborn red staining that the sauce leaves in your plastic food-storage containers. So here's a tip from some wise old country grandmas: Before storing any kind of tomato-based food or sauce in a plastic container, rub the inside of the container with vegetable oil to form a protective barrier against stains. (Applying a thin coating of vegetable-oil cooking spray will work, too.)

A good way to remove stubborn food odors (like that of onions) from plastic containers without spending a penny is to crumple a piece of newspaper into the clean, dry container; secure the lid tightly; and leave it until morning. Then remove the paper to take the odor away.

Get rid of odors on wooden bowls, wooden salad utensils, and wooden cutting boards by rubbing the surface with the cut side of a lemon.

Baking soda is also great for cleaning and deodorizing wooden surfaces. Mix ½ cup baking soda with a quart of warm water, and use a clean sponge to rub it on the wood surface. Rinse with plain water, blot with a clean towel, and allow to air dry completely. You can then bring back the wood's natural finish by coating it with boiled linseed or vegetable oil and using fine steel wool to rub the oil in. Apply a couple more coats of oil 24 hours apart, wiping off the excess between each application.

Remove stains from woodenware with a mild bleach solution (¼ cup bleach to 1 quart warm water). Then rinse and dry before reapplying a protective coating of oil (as described in the preceding hint).

When it's time to wash your treasured family heirlooms, such as that personalized anniversary plate or your great-great-grandmother's delicate glass hummingbird collection, avoid accidental chips and breakage by padding the bottom of the sink with a thick towel and wrapping a second towel or washcloth around the faucet. Never use strong chemicals, abrasive cleansers, or steel-wool pads. Warm water—with a small amount of mild dish soap (not the antibacterial variety) if absolutely necessary—and gentle wiping with a soft cloth, sponge, or just your fingertips will typically do the trick with the least risk to your valuables. Do not wash delicate pieces in the dishwasher or in a sink filled with other dishes; wash them by hand, one by one.

To remove calcium deposits from a glass vase or a glass coffee- or teapot, scrub with the flesh of a lemon (it's fine to use a lemon wedge that has already been squeezed or that has floated in a glass or pitcher of water, by the way). You can sprinkle on a little baking soda or salt to help rub away really stubborn stains.

To scrub away calcium deposits from the inside of a narrow-necked vase, combine a little white vinegar and

Hot Cleaning Tip!

Boiling has been used through the ages as a standard way to disinfect clothing, bedding, tools, and more. It's just as useful today. Kitchen sponges and dish rags, for example, are breeding grounds for a host of disease-causing germs, but you can disinfect them by boiling them in water for several minutes every few days. Also, allow them to dry out thoroughly between uses by having two and alternating between them.

uncooked rice in the vase and swish them around vigor-ously. Then pour them out and wash the vase as usual.

Coat oven spills and splashes with salt as soon as possible after they occur. (But be careful! Wear an oven mitt and use a long-handled spoon to sprinkle salt on harder-to-reach spills.) Once the oven has cooled down, use a damp rag or sponge to easily wipe them away.

Patience: Nature's Scrub Brush

You've no doubt heard sayings like "Good things come to those who wait" and "Time heals all wounds." Well, don't underestimate the benefits of a little patience when it comes to cleaning dishware and cookware. You're much less likely to need a potentially damaging abrasive scrubber or powerful chemical detergent if you simply allow your dirty plates, bowls, pots, and pans to soak in hot, sudsy water for 15 to 30 minutes before you attempt to clean them. A good soak will usually make even the toughest caked-on food particles wipe away easily. Matter of fact, some of the gunk will slide off by itself. So try slowing down a bit. Fill the sink with dishes, hot water, and suds, then spend some time with your family while nature does some of the work for you.

If your icebox has taken on some not-so-pleasant odors, it's probably time for a good cleaning. First, check all the bottles, containers, and foods and toss out any that are beyond their "use by" date. (Sometimes that's enough to cure a stink problem.) Next, thoroughly wipe down the walls, shelves, and other surfaces inside the fridge with a damp sponge sprinkled with baking soda. Finally, rinse and wring out the sponge, moisten it with white vinegar, and wipe down the rubber seals and any other areas in the icebox that are prone to mildew growth.

To help absorb potent or unpleasant food aromas in your icebox, try soaking a cotton ball in vanilla (be sure to use real vanilla extract) and putting it on a small ceramic plate or in a small, shallow, glass or ceramic bowl in a corner of the fridge.

Help absorb the odor of fish during cooking by setting out a small glass bowl or shallow glass dish of bleach. Place the bowl in an out-of-the-way spot on a counter or table in the kitchen so that you won't knock into it and splash the bleach onto your clothes or into food. Also be sure it's out of the reach of kids and pets. Then, when you're washing up after the meal, carefully pour the bleach down the kitchen drain to deodorize it, too.

To clean splatters and spots from a ceramic-tile backsplash, wipe it down with a clean sponge dampened with rubbing alcohol. The rubbing alcohol will not only get rid of the gunk, it will disinfect the backsplash, too.

To mask odors from trash, place fresh lemon or orange peels in the bottom of your garbage pail. Replace as needed to keep the container sweeter smelling.

Another way to keep garbage pails smelling better is to sprinkle borax into the bottom. Change the borax when it no longer seems to be doing the job.

METALS

To remove tarnish from a copper-bottomed pan or pot, turn the cookware upside down, wet the copper surface with white vinegar, sprinkle on some salt, scrub with a clean rag or paper towel, and rinse. Didn't get all the tarnish? Just repeat the process until the entire copper bottom shines like a brand-new penny.

A quick and handy way to do some touch-up cleaning of copper and brass is to slice a lemon in half (cutting it lengthwise will probably give you a slightly larger cleaning surface), sprinkle the flesh of one half with salt, and then, grasping the lemon by the peel, use the salted flesh to scrub away spots of tarnish.

Versatile Vinegar

In addition to the many ways vinegar has been used in cleaning, it has long been a staple of both kitchen pantries and—believe it or not—medicine chests. During the Civil War and World War I, for example, military medics used vinegar to treat wounds. And folk-medicine traditions from all across the United States and around the world have put vinegar to use for relieving a wide variety of ills—from age spots, dry hair, and diarrhea to insect bites, sore throats, and sunburn.

Silver candlesticks that have hardened wax drippings on them can be cleaned without damage to their finish if you first put them in the freezer. Once the wax freezes, it can be easily peeled away. For any stubborn wax remnants, cover your fingernail or a wooden craft stick with a soft cloth and use it to gently scrape the bits away.

Plain old generic toothpaste (the gritty paste variety, not the fancy gel form) makes a great inexpensive silver polish. Use it the same as you would commercial silver polish to restore shine.

After juicing a lemon for a recipe or beverage, don't just toss the remnants into the trash. Holding a lemon half (or wedge) by the peel side, rub the flesh over a faucet blemished with calcium (water) stains to remove them.

Rubbing with the flesh of a cut lemon is also a great way to make aluminum shine.

Prior to painting, clean metal objects by wiping the surface with a solution of 1 part vinegar and 5 parts water. Including this prep step will help to prevent peeling of your new paint job.

WALLS

To clean wallpaper, gently brush off all loose dirt and dust. Then remove the crust from a slice or hunk of white or rye bread, wad up the soft center, and use it as a natural eraser to gently rub off smears and stuck-on soil.

Nasty grease spots speckling your kitchen wallpaper? Remove them by laying a few sheets of blotting paper against the spots and holding a hot iron close to the wall. Wear an oven mitt on your hand to protect your fingers as you hold the blotting paper in place against the wall. The special paper will slowly absorb the grease spots from the wallpaper. Just be sure not to press the iron directly against the wallpaper.

The following recipe makes a good, inexpensive cleaner for painted walls: Mix ½ cup vinegar, 1 cup clear ammonia, ¼ cup baking soda, and 1 gallon warm water. Apply to the wall with a sponge, and rinse with plain water. Because this cleaner contains ammonia, you should wear rubber or vinyl gloves when applying it and make sure the room you are working in is well ventilated.

Remove scuff marks from painted walls and from the painted risers between stairs by scrubbing with a rag that's been dampened with rubbing alcohol.

Blot It Out!

Blotting paper is a useful item to have on hand for removing greasy spots from a variety of surfaces around your home. Blotting paper is special absorbent paper that was traditionally used to sop up excess ink left on paper from old-fashioned fountain pens. Fashionable ladies also used small sheets of it to absorb excess amounts of natural skin oil on the face. These days, it can still be found where writing and art supplies are sold as well as in the cosmetics section of drugstores and variety stores.

Another option for ridding painted walls of scuff marks is to scrub the scuffs with old-fashioned toothpaste (not the gel variety that's so common today) on an old, soft-bristled toothbrush.

To clean and polish woodwork that has an oil finish, try this trick: First, pour equal parts turpentine and boiled linseed oil (available at hardware or paint stores) in a jar, tighten the lid, and shake until the liquid is blended thoroughly. Then, pour a small amount of the mix onto a soft cloth, and rub it into the woodwork in the direction of the wood's grain. The surface will at first look oily, but within an hour the polish will be completely absorbed, leaving a lovely, soft shine.

WINDOWS & MIRRORS

Don't waste money on expensive commercial glass cleaners when you can easily mix up excellent and highly effective glass cleaners at home for less. For windows that really need a good clean (as well as for mirrors, glass panels on furniture, and the like), combine 2 tablespoons ammonia, ½ cup rubbing alcohol, and ¼ teaspoon of mild (not antibacterial) dishwashing liquid. Using a funnel, pour the mixture into a recycled spray bottle (be sure the original contents have been thoroughly rinsed out and that the bottle has been allowed to dry out before reusing it). Then spray it on windows just as you would commercial glass cleaner, and wipe. Be careful not to get the solution in your eyes, and be sure to clearly mark the spray bottle with its new contents.

 For quick, touch-up cleaning of glass, combine 2 tablespoons vinegar per cup of water in a spray bottle. Use as you would commercial window cleaner.

 When it's window-cleaning time, turn lint and unsightly streaks and smears into yesterday's news by spraying the windows with homemade glass cleaner (see the recipes above) and wiping them dry using crumpled-up newspaper. Employing newsprint instead of rags or paper towels will leave your hands dirty but your windows sparkling and lint-free, cheaply and without streaks. You can also dip the crumpled newspaper directly into a bucket of the homemade cleaner (wear rubber or vinyl gloves if you do this with the ammonia-based cleaner recipe), wipe down the glass with the wet newspaper, and, to finish off, use dry sheets of newspaper to dry and polish the windows.

 A slightly more modern alternative to cleaning mirrors or windows with newspaper—one that's also convenient, inexpensive, and lint-free but won't leave your hands coated in ink—is to use paper coffee filters. That's right. They're cheap and absorbent and won't leave your windows with a fuzzy coat.

There's the Rub

Isopropyl, or rubbing, alcohol has a variety of household uses in addition to its role as a disinfectant for wounds. But like all alcohols, it has a tendency to dry out the skin. To protect your hands, therefore, you may want to don rubber or vinyl gloves when using tips that call for rubbing alcohol.

Did your teacher ever assign you to stay after school to pound the dust out of the blackboard erasers? For young children, getting assigned that task was an honor. For older ones, it was usually a punishment for misbehaving in class. Now that you're an adult, one of those old-fashioned blackboard erasers may once again leave you proud, as you look out through crystal-clear windows. After washing and drying your windows, run a clean, dry blackboard eraser over them to remove any streaks and give them a diamond-bright shine.

Remove paint splatters from windows using a clean cloth dampened with hot vinegar. Heat the vinegar in a small pot on the stove. Be careful not to heat the vinegar to boiling, and wear rubber or vinyl dishwashing gloves to protect your fingers from the hot liquid.

No matter which supplies you use, avoid cleaning windows when the sun is shining directly on the glass or when there's a warm, dry wind. The sun and wind will dry the cleaner before you've had a chance to wipe the window clean, leaving behind spots, streaks, and film, not to mention a lot of the dirt you meant to clean off in the first place.

If, after you've cleaned your windows or other glass items, you discover tiny scratches, eliminate them by polishing them with toothpaste (be sure it's paste and not gel) and an old toothbrush or clean terry-cloth rag.

Next time you change the windshield-wiper blades on your car or truck, save the old ones to use as squeegees on the windows of your home.

Wipe This Way

When cleaning windows, use only vertical strokes on the outside and only horizontal ones on the inside, or vice versa. This way, you will be able to quickly determine whether any streaks are on the inside or outside of the windows.

LAUNDRY

❖ ❖ ❖ ❖

While you don't need to return to the days of hand-washing every piece of clothing or scrubbing grime and stains out with the aid of a washboard (although a small washboard *can* really come in handy when you're trying to remove set-in grass stains from a pair of jeans), taking advantage of the following old-fashioned, low-cost, tried-and-true laundry tips may end up turning your wash day(s) into much less of a chore.

To boost the cleaning and deodorizing powers of your usual laundry detergent, add ½ cup borax to each load. You'll find borax in the laundry aisle of your local grocery or variety store.

 Your delicate washables can be safely and effectively laundered in warm water to which you've added a small amount of mild dishwashing liquid (not the fancy anti-bacterial variety).

 Club soda, used straight from the bottle, is a great emergency spot cleaner and stain remover. Apply it with a clean, damp cloth.

 Grass stains on clothes can be removed with an old toothbrush and plain white toothpaste; just make sure you use a paste variety and not a gel. Squeeze a small amount of the toothpaste onto the stain, then dip the toothbrush in clean water and use it to scrub away the stain. Repeat this process as needed to treat all of the stain(s). Then rinse the area and launder the clothing as usual.

To remove spots of blood from clothing, use 3 percent hydrogen peroxide (the kind you find in the first-aid section of the store). Soak the stain with the peroxide, use your fingernail or the blade of a butter knife to help loosen and scrape away the blood, then rinse it away with more hydrogen peroxide. In most cases, you'll have better luck removing stains—especially blood stains—if you treat them immediately after they happen, before the stains have a chance to dry.

Storing & Using Hydrogen Peroxide

Hydrogen peroxide is typically sold in the first-aid section of stores as a 3 percent solution that has mild antiseptic and bleaching effects. It is safe for most fibers, although it's always best to spot-test in an inconspicuous area. (The higher-percent and thus more potent peroxide solution used for lightening hair is too strong to use safely on fabric and other household surfaces.) Buy hydrogen peroxide in small quantities and store it in a cool, dark place in its original opaque container; it loses strength quickly after it is opened and if it is exposed to light.

Another method for removing blood from clothing is to wet the stained area of the fabric with water, sprinkle it with plain old table salt, rub one half of the stain against the other to work in the salt and loosen the stain, then immediately launder the garment the way you usually do.

 You don't need a special stain remover or laundry pre-treater to banish ring around the collar. Whether it's on work shirts or Sunday best, staining around the collar can be easily vanquished with a bit of shampoo. It makes perfect sense when you think about it: The oil and sweat that build up on shirt collars are really no different than the oil and sweat from your scalp that accumulate on your hair and make it look greasy. Just pour a little shampoo— any shampoo will do, even an inexpensive generic—onto the collar, rub the collar together to work the shampoo in well, and rinse thoroughly. Then launder as usual. (A modern-day twist on this traditional tip: The next time you stay at a motel or hotel, be sure to bring home those little complimentary bottles of shampoo supplied for guests, especially if you don't much care for the scent or quality. Think of them as convenient little packages of ring-around-the-collar remover!)

 To remove lipstick from dark fabrics, take a piece of white bread and remove the crust, then wad up the soft center and rub it gently on the stain until it picks up all of the lipstick. Sweep away any leftover crumbs with a clean, soft-bristled brush.

A Real "Fresh Scent"

So many laundry products sold today advertise their ability to leave your clothes, bedding, and towels with the "fresh scent" of this or that—from cherry blossoms and honeysuckle to ocean breezes and spring showers. To infuse fabric with such aromas, manufacturers use a variety of chemicals, both natural and artificial. But not a single one truly reproduces the crisp, comforting smell of laundry that has been freshly dried outdoors. So try giving your senses a treat by drying your laundry the old-fashioned country way: When weather and space permit, hang a load of just-washed clothes (or at least your towels and washcloths) outside on a laundry line or drying rack. You're sure to be pleasantly surprised when you discover the scent that fresh air really gives to fabrics.

For stubborn stains on flannel fabric, pour 1 egg yolk and 1 tablespoon glycerine into a deep, wide-mouthed plastic cup; mix them together using a fork, the way you whisk milk into raw eggs to make scrambled eggs; and smear the mixture onto the stain. Wait about 30 minutes for it to loosen the stain, then launder the item as usual. (You can usually find glycerine in drugstores, at hobby and craft stores, and with the cake-decorating supplies in the baking aisle of many grocery stores.)

 Lift a fresh grease spot from fabric by sprinkling the spot with cornstarch. Allow the cornstarch to soak up the grease for a few minutes, and then brush it away.

 Oily stains on pillowcases can be removed with plain shampoo. Just pour some on the stained areas, rub it in, rinse thoroughly, and launder the pillowcases as usual.

 To help make the fabric of new pillowcases more resistant to stains from natural skin oils and oily hair products, starch it lightly before use.

If you get ink on a piece of clothing, try soaking the ink mark with rubbing alcohol and wiping it away with a clean, white cloth.

 Another old-fashioned remedy for removing ink marks from clothes and other fabrics is to wet a sponge with milk and rub the ink stain until it disappears.

 To remove tea stains from clothing or table linens, submerge the stained area for several minutes in a small container of heavily sugared water (stir the water as you

Hang 'Em High

If you'll be drying clothes on an outdoor clothesline, first be sure the line itself is clean. Then use clean clothespins to attach items to the line by their sturdiest edges. Dry white and light-colored fabrics in direct sun to take advantage of the sun's natural bleaching action. To protect dark- or bright-colored clothes while they dry, hang them out of direct sunlight. Smooth the clothes as you hang them, running your fingers down seams and hand-straightening collars and cuffs. Oh, and of course, be sure to check that the line is high enough, or the clothes are pinned in such a way, that none of your just-washed clothes are touching the ground.

add sugar to it, and keep adding sugar until it no longer dissolves). Then launder as usual.

 To really brighten a white tablecloth, fill a large pot with water to which you've added a sliced-up lemon, peels and all. Bring the water to a boil, then remove the pot from the heat. Add the tablecloth to the pot, let it soak for about an hour, then remove it from the pot and launder it as usual. You might consider hanging the tablecloth outside on a laundry line to dry, as well, since sunlight naturally bleaches white fabrics.

 To brighten smaller white-linen items such as napkins and handkerchiefs, first wash them as you usually do, then soak them overnight in a sink or tub of water to which you've mixed in a small amount of cream of tartar. Rinse the linens with plain water and, if possible, hang them in the sun to dry (or simply dry them as usual).

 You can make your own quick spray starch at home by slowly adding ½ teaspoon cornstarch and 1½ teaspoons wheat starch to 1 cup cold water. Stir until all of the starch is dissolved, and then pour the mixture into a clean spray bottle. Use it as needed to spray fabrics lightly when you iron them.

 If you've accidentally scorched an item of clothing while ironing it, hang it on a laundry line in direct sunlight; sunlight's natural bleaching action will help to fade the scorch mark.

 Here's a tip for dulling the unsightly shine that often develops on the seat of dark pants. After laundering as usual, spray the shiny area with vinegar and, without rinsing out the vinegar, allow it to dry before wearing.

 To remove tobacco odors from wool clothing, run hot water into the bathtub and add 2 cups white vinegar. Then hang the garment on the shower rod and close the bathroom door. The vinegar in the rising steam will remove the smell of smoke without damaging the fabric.

If you spray new canvas tennis shoes with starch before wearing them, dirt can't become embedded in the fabric and the shoes will always be easy to clean.

Ridding shoes of dampness from foot perspiration can help prevent odor and even lengthen the life of the shoes. So whenever you take off a pair of shoes for the day, slip a few small pieces of white chalk into each shoe to help absorb moisture. Remnants of inexpensive children's sidewalk chalk will work just fine, too. For a tidy, efficient way to move the chalk pieces into and out of your shoes, consider wrapping them in small scraps of cheesecloth and tying the tiny bundles with twist ties or slipping them into the toe ends of old knee-high nylon stockings

Ironing Board Cover-up

Tired of wrestling with an ironing-board cover that just doesn't fit properly and keeps sliding off or creasing up under your fabrics? Give that cover a near-perfect fit by placing it in the proper position on the ironing board (and securing its ties or straps) while it's still damp from the washer and letting it dry in place.

and knotting the openings. Whether you use loose bits of chalk or these little homemade shoe sachets, be sure you remember to remove them before you slip your feet back into the shoes!

 Another easy way to help remove moisture from the inside of shoes is to crumple up newspaper and stuff it inside between wearings. Be sure to use fresh pieces of newspaper each time.

 For a homemade lint remover, roll up an old magazine or thin mail-order catalog and wrap wide adhesive tape around it so the sticky side faces out. Pass it lightly over clothing or upholstery fabric to remove lint, bits of thread, and stray hairs.

PEST CONTROL

❖ ❖ ❖

Seems that no matter how much progress we humans make, we still can't outrun the pests and pesky varmints that have plagued our kind for generations. The battle between "us" and "them" continues to this day. But that doesn't mean we can't learn a thing or two from folks who lived far closer to nature than most of us do today. Their creative defenses, some of which are described in this chapter, at least kept the fight a draw. So we'd be fools to ignore them, especially since our modern-day antipest weapons haven't exactly won us the war.

INDOOR INVASIONS

 If you discover that ants have invaded your home, try sprinkling ground cinnamon in the areas where you see them, especially along baseboards and into any cracks and crevices that may be serving as their entry points, highways, or home bases.

 Some folks have had success at repelling red ants by placing sprigs of fresh, aromatic, garden sage in the cabinet or pantry where they store sugar, honey, molasses, and other ant-attracting sweet staples. Dried sage leaves may also work: Simply wrap some of the dried herb in small pieces of cheesecloth or muslin, use twist ties to secure the bundles, and place these sage sachets on the shelves in your pantry or cabinet.

 Bay leaves placed in cupboards can also help discourage ants and other creepy crawlies from settling in.

 The potent smell of cloves often proves an effective deterrent to roaches and ants. Try laying a tiny trail of whole cloves along baseboards and near doors. Put some in kitchen cabinets and drawers, too, if you find the invaders there as well.

Cucumber peels are said to be useful in fighting cockroach infestations. And they're certainly far less toxic than modern chemical roach controllers. So before you go to bed, spread fresh peels at the edges of the floor along the

Sweep away Pests

Perhaps the surest way to rid your home of pesky invaders such as ants, roaches, mice, and rats, as well as the best way to prevent their return, is to remove their primary reason for coming to live with you in the first place. That means taking away their source(s) of food. Be religious about sweeping up food crumbs, including bits of pet food, from open areas *and* from those hidden nooks and crannies on floors, countertops, and cupboard shelves. Frequently clean beneath and behind your large kitchen appliances. Refrigerate whatever foods you can (store white, brown, and powdered sugars in resealable bags or containers in the icebox, for example), and place all unrefrigerated edibles in sealed containers—metal ones if rodents are a problem. Take these basic steps, and you'll be well on your way to evicting the pesky varmints.

baseboards, on the bottom shelves of low cabinets, and around drains. Come morning, remove the peels. Put down fresh peels for three nights in a row to help chase roaches from your home.

 To kill ants or roaches indoors, sprinkle borax onto a dollop of jam, mix together thoroughly, then spoon a bit of the mixture into soda-bottle caps. Place the caps under appliances and sinks and in the back corners of cabinets where they will be safely out of the reach of children and pets. The sweet but toxic borax-spiked jam should kill any creepy crawlies that ingest it.

 Protect your pasta, rice, cereals, and other grains from mealworms by placing a few wrapped sticks of sugar-free spearmint chewing gum on the shelves where you store these kitchen staples. Apparently, mealworms just can't tolerate that minty fresh scent. And because it doesn't contain sugar, the gum itself shouldn't attract any ants, either. When the sticks of gum start to lose their spearmint smell, replace them with fresh sticks.

Send Moths Packing

Who wouldn't love to have a cedar-lined closet? The cedar repels moths and makes the closet and clothes inside it smell wonderful. But installing such a lining takes time, effort, money, and know-how. Fortunately, you can enjoy the benefits of cedar without rebuilding your clothes closet. Take a handful of cedar chips or cedar bedding (the kind sold for pet cages), place it in the center of a piece of muslin, gather the edges of the fabric, twist, and close with a twist tie or piece of ribbon, yarn, or string. Then hang this homemade cedar sachet in your closet. It's an easy, inexpensive, and sweet-smelling way to keep moths at bay.

 Prevent weevils from settling into your flour and grain products by tucking a dried chili pepper into each bag or container. The peppers won't alter the taste of these foods but should repel those nasty weevils.

 Make your home a little too hot and spicy for mice by filling a watering can with 2 gallons of water and mixing in 1 cup mild dishwashing liquid (the kind that doesn't contain antibacterial agents) and 2 tablespoons of hot sauce (the hotter the better). Sprinkle the solution around the perimeter of your home, especially around doorways; mix more solution as needed.

 If mice have managed to find their way into your home and settled in, sprinkle dried, ground, hot (cayenne) pepper into any mouse holes that you find. Also liberally sprinkle this natural rodent repellent in areas where you frequently spot mice or find their droppings.

OUTDOOR ATTACKS

 Erect a tiny roadblock if you spot a line of ants parading their way toward your home. Just pour a thin line of all-purpose flour across their path, which should cause them to scatter and, hopefully, regroup elsewhere, away from your home. To lay the line, take a piece of paper, wrap one end tightly around a thin knitting needle or barbecue skewer, tape the edge of the paper to itself to hold it in this funnel shape, and slowly fill the makeshift funnel with the flour. (Of course, if you happen to have a tiny funnel or cake-decorating tool with a narrow nozzle, you can use it instead to pour your miniature wall of flour.)

Keep Crawling Invaders Out

To help keep ants from invading your home, thoroughly combine 2 cups borax and 1 cup white flour and pour the mixture into a clean, dry, quart-size jar that has a screw-on lid. Punch multiple holes in the lid, then screw it onto the jar. Sprinkle this powdery deterrent in a narrow swath against the outside of your house's foundation. Borax can be a skin or respiratory irritant and can be toxic if ingested in large enough amounts, however, so you may need to prevent curious little fingers or paws from coming into contact with it. One way to do this: Cut narrow strips of chicken wire; curl each strip lengthwise into a half-moon shape with a diameter wide enough to cover the borax swath; then lay them, end-to-end, over the powder, with one long side propped against the house and the other long side pushed about an inch into the soil along the outer edge of the borax swath. Refresh your borax border as needed, especially after a heavy rain.

Holding the filled funnel above the ant parade, slowly slide the needle or skewer out. As the flour pours from the narrow end, trace a solid line in the shape of an arrow's head, with the tip crossing the ants' path and the sides extending outward diagonally, away from your house.

If you're worried that ants that have built mounds near your home's foundation will make their way into your abode, try sprinkling their ant hills with cornmeal or dry grits. These grains absorb a lot of moisture and rapidly expand, so once the tiny ants consume them, well, they most likely won't need another meal—ever.

 To quickly evict ants from ant mounds near your home, simply saturate their hills with lemon juice.

 To help prevent skunks from taking up residence beneath your porch, under or around your house, or anywhere else on your property that puts these little stinkers a little too close for your olfactory comfort, fight fire with fire (or, in this case, odor with odor). Take several rags, rip them into strips, generously sprinkle the strips with cheap perfume (eau de cologne, toilet water, or even potent aftershave will do just fine), and tuck them around the areas you want to defend. Apparently our odoriferous black-and-white friends don't like our pretty perfume any more than we appreciate theirs!

Slugs are stubborn, slimy garden munchers that especially favor greens and the tender leaves of young plants, and few remedies control them completely. But to help give your garden a fighting chance against them, try rinsing, drying, and crushing up eggshells and then spreading them thickly around vulnerable plants. Mound them up against the stalks, too. The sharp edges of the shells can apparently make life difficult for the slippery little slugs. The eggshells also act as fantastic natural fertilizer for your garden soil, so when you put your garden to bed at the end of the growing season, just turn the all-natural eggshell mulch directly into the dirt.

Another reportedly helpful technique for discouraging slugs from feeding in your garden is to spread coffee grounds on the soil surface. Place a thick layer of grounds around the base of plants, especially lettuce and young plants with tender leaves, which are slug favorites. Like eggshells, the coffee grounds help to enrich the soil and can be mixed into the dirt when you turn over your garden beds at the end of the season.

If birds are hindering your attempts at growing your own leaf lettuce, try screening them out. Make a wooden frame that's just slightly larger than your lettuce patch, staple window screening to it, pound stakes into the soil at the corners of the lettuce patch to prop your screened frame just a few inches above the soil, and lay the frame on top of them. (Of course, if you have or can find some old, ready-made window screens of the appropriate size, all the better.) Your homemade shield will let sun and water in but help keep most of the thieving birds—as well as some other hungry pests—away from the seeds and the tasty lettuce leaves.

Squirrels, birds, rabbits, and deer tend to scatter at sharp, sudden sounds. If these critters have been helping themselves to the produce in your vegetable garden (or the bulbs and seeds in your flower beds), try sticking a few 3-foot-high wooden poles or dowels into the dirt throughout your garden and using string to attach an aluminum pie plate to each one. (Use a thumbtack to pin one end of the string near the top of the pole, punch a hole in the pie plate, run the loose end of the string through the hole, and tie off the plate so that it hangs about midway down the pole.) With even a slight breeze, the pans will rattle against the poles and help scare away garden invaders.

 Mice, rats, squirrels, and other little varmints seem to find the smell of peppermint offensive. Fortunately, to most people, the peppermint aroma is quite pleasant. So to help make your yard less tempting to these destructive critters, try growing some peppermint. Mint plants do have a tendency to spread on their own, however, so if you don't want them crowding out your other flowers and plants, consider planting them in large containers. Then simply intersperse these planters among the other plants growing around your yard.

QUICK FIXES & HANDY TIPS

❖ ❖ ❖ ❖

From loosening stuck nuts and bolts to shining shoes and perking up a sagging bouquet of flowers, generations of country folk had to come up with all sorts of practical, creative answers and fast, frugal fixes. Employing do-it-yourself solutions was often the only way they *could* tackle the little challenges of daily living away from the specialized stores and services found in cities. Now you, too, can save time and money by helping yourself to some of their wise ways of solving common household problems.

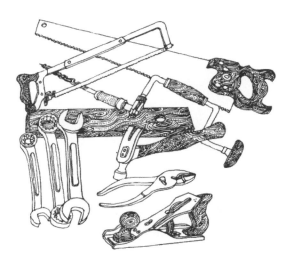

If a zipper keeps getting stuck, take a dry bar of soap and rub it up and down the zipper's teeth.

Limit wax drippings by popping candles into the refrigerator for a few hours prior to lighting them. If you have the space, consider storing some in the icebox in a sealed container—to minimize the spread of any fragrance from the wax to your foods, or vice versa—so they're ready whenever you need them.

Do you like the smell of a certain kind of bar soap? Tuck a new bar, with its box or paper wrapper still on, into a dresser drawer to lend the pleasant scent to your clothes.

Rubbing alcohol is great for removing mildew on shoes, luggage, and similar items that don't go into the washing machine. Dampen a clean rag with the alcohol, and wipe the mildewed area with it. If the mildew is more deeply set in, place the item in a bathtub or basin and carefully pour rubbing alcohol onto the affected area. (It's always safest to spot-test this treatment on a small, inconspicuous area of the item first, though, to be sure it doesn't cause fading or staining.)

 There's no monkey business here, just a quick, convenient, low-cost way to give dark-colored leather shoes and boots a shine. Eat a banana, then rub the inside of the banana peel on the leather to polish it. Finish off by buffing the footwear with a soft, dry cloth.

 To remove ink or marker from your hands (or any other spot of skin, for that matter), pour a little plain tomato juice on a cloth, and use it to rub away the mark.

 To remove adhesive from your skin or clothing, soak the area in lemon juice, then rub the sticky stuff away.

A Truly Handy Measure

Precisely measure the width of your hand with your thumb and fingers spread, commit the number to memory, and you'll be able to make rough measurements without a ruler or tape measure.

A dash or two of vodka added to the water in a vase of fresh-cut flowers will help prevent algae growth in the water and keep your flowers perky longer.

 To sharpen scissors or garden shears, use them to slice up a piece of sandpaper that's been folded several times with the rough side out.

 To soften hardened paintbrush bristles, soak them in hot vinegar, then use a wire brush to separate them and to remove remnants of varnish or paint.

 A thick rubber band wrapped around the plastic handle of a screwdriver will help improve your grip and make tightening and loosening screws easier.

 You may be able to quiet annoying squeaks in your wood floors by dusting talcum powder into the cracks between the floorboards.

 There's no need to resort to pricey commercial lubricants to quiet a squeaking door hinge. A bit of generic vegetable oil squirted or dripped onto the moving parts will do the job just as well. Generic vegetable-oil cooking spray is handy for this problem, too.

 If you have a cabinet or dresser drawer that sticks, take a bar of soap and run it along the drawer's rail(s). Rubbing an old candle along the rails will also work.

 A thin coating of olive oil will help ease the movement of a key that tends to stick in the lock.

 A light dusting of talcum powder on a stubbornly tight knot in a shoelace or other fabric string can make it easier to loosen and untie.

 You can make screws easier to insert by twisting them into a bar of soap first.

 If a screw is so loose that it is barely or no longer gripping (but you can't reposition it and drill a new hole), remove it, wrap its threads with a few strands of very fine wire or fine steel wool, then screw it back into its old hole.

If a screw has been ripped out of its hole and the hole is now too big for the screw threads to gain hold, try sliding a wooden match into the hole and screwing in the fastener once more.

Don't take a chance of hitting your thumb or finger when hammering a small brad, tack, or nail. Slip the fastener between the teeth of a pocket comb first. The comb then holds the fastener while you hold the comb, keeping your fingers out of harm's way when you bring that hammer down. A bobby pin, paper clip, or tweezers can be used in place of the comb as well.

When attempting to hammer a nail in a tight or hard-to-reach area, try using a bit of modeling clay (or, in a pinch, a wad of chewed gum) to help hold the nail in place for the first couple of hammer blows.

To help loosen rusty nuts and bolts, pour cola, 3 percent hydrogen peroxide, or lemon juice over them and wait half an hour for the liquid to eat away at the rust enough for the fastener to turn freely.

Loosen a stubborn screw, bolt, or nut from a metal surface with white vinegar, kerosene, or ammonia. Careful, though: Kerosene is flammable, so it should not be used near an open flame, and working safely with ammonia requires good ventilation.

Homemade Rust Fighter

To make a rust-preventive coating for tools, outdoor furniture, and other metal objects: Combine ¼ cup lanolin and 1 cup petroleum jelly in a double boiler over low heat. Stir until the ingredients have melted and are thoroughly blended, then remove the mixture from the heat, pour it into a clean glass jar with a lid, and let it partially cool. Using a clean rag or cheap paintbrush, apply the mixture while it's still warm, and don't wipe it off—simply allow it to dry on the object. If there's any of the mixture left over, cover the jar tightly with the lid for storage, then rewarm the mixture just before you use it again. Coat tools and outdoor furniture at least once a year, in early spring, touching up the coating as needed. If you're in a pinch and don't have any of this homemade coating prepared, you can help protect new metal tools from rust by smearing a thin layer of petroleum jelly on them before you use them or take them outdoors for the first time.

If you don't have a carpenter's level, substitute a tall, straight-sided jar (like the kind green olives often come in) with a tight-fitting lid. Fill the jar three-quarters full of water. Lay it on its side on the surface you're testing, but keep a hand on it so it doesn't roll off and shatter on the ground. When the water is level, the surface is, too.

If a lightbulb has broken off in a socket, grab a bar of soap, press it gently but firmly into the portion of the bulb remaining in the socket, and use it to unscrew the remnant. For safety's sake, you should cut the electrical power to the socket first.

A piece of children's sidewalk chalk or a charcoal briquet (but not the kind pretreated with lighter fluid) slipped into a toolbox or tackle box will help absorb moisture and prevent rusting.

To help prevent humidity or moisture from clumping the salt in your saltshaker, add several grains of uncooked rice to the container.

101
OLD-TIME
COUNTRY
Household Hints

Publications International, Ltd.

ISBN-13: 978-1-4127-7112-2
ISBN-10: 1-4127-7112-9

Manufactured in China.

8 7 6 5 4 3 2 1